55 Pie Recipes for Home

By: Kelly Johnson

Table of Contents

Pies:

- Classic Apple Pie
- Blueberry-Lemon Pie
- Chocolate Silk Pie
- Cherry Almond Pie
- Pecan Pie
- Banana Cream Pie
- Key Lime Pie
- Caramel Apple Crumble Pie
- Raspberry White Chocolate Pie
- Coconut Cream Pie
- Strawberry Rhubarb Pie
- Blackberry Galette
- Lemon Meringue Pie
- Maple Pecan Pumpkin Pie
- Triple Berry Pie
- Chocolate Peanut Butter Pie
- Sweet Potato Pie
- Peach Bourbon Hand Pies
- Oreo Cheesecake Pie
- Cinnamon Roll Apple Pie
- S'mores Pie
- Espresso Chocolate Pie
- Fig and Honey Tart
- Caramel Pecan CHocolate Pie
- Lemon Blueberry Chess Pie
- Raspberry Chocolate Ganache Tart
- Buttermilk Pie
- Apple Cranberry Walnut Tart
- Bourbon CHocolate Pecan Pie
- Caramel Banana Cream Pie
- Pear and Gorgonzola Galette
- CHocolate Mint Grasshopper Pie
- Strawberry Basil Mascarpone Tart
- Coconut Lime Icebox Pie
- Cinnamon Apple Crustless Pie

Classic Apple Pie

Ingredients:

For the Pie Crust:

- 2 1/2 cups all-purpose flour
- 1 cup unsalted butter, chilled and cut into small cubes
- 1 teaspoon salt
- 1 tablespoon granulated sugar
- 6-8 tablespoons ice water

For the Apple Filling:

- 6-7 cups peeled, cored, and thinly sliced apples (a mix of Granny Smith and Honeycrisp works well)
- 3/4 cup granulated sugar
- 1/4 cup light brown sugar, packed
- 1 teaspoon ground cinnamon
- 1/4 teaspoon ground nutmeg
- 2 tablespoons all-purpose flour
- 1 tablespoon lemon juice
- 1 teaspoon vanilla extract

For Assembly:

- 1 tablespoon unsalted butter, cut into small pieces (for dotting on top)
- 1 egg (for egg wash)
- 1 tablespoon milk (for egg wash)
- Additional sugar for sprinkling

Instructions:

1. Make the Pie Crust:

- In a large bowl, combine the flour, salt, and sugar. Add the chilled butter cubes and use a pastry cutter or your hands to mix until the mixture resembles coarse crumbs.
- Gradually add ice water, one tablespoon at a time, until the dough just comes together.

- Divide the dough in half, shape each half into a disk, wrap in plastic wrap, and refrigerate for at least 1 hour.

2. Prepare the Apple Filling:

- In a large bowl, toss the sliced apples with lemon juice to prevent browning.
- In a separate bowl, mix together granulated sugar, brown sugar, cinnamon, nutmeg, and flour.
- Add the sugar mixture to the apples, tossing until evenly coated. Stir in vanilla extract.

3. Roll Out the Pie Crust:

- Preheat the oven to 425°F (220°C).
- Roll out one disk of pie crust on a lightly floured surface to fit a 9-inch pie dish. Transfer the crust to the pie dish.

4. Fill the Pie:

- Pour the prepared apple filling into the pie crust, mounding it slightly in the center. Dot the filling with small pieces of butter.

5. Add the Top Crust:

- Roll out the second disk of pie crust and place it over the apples. Trim any excess crust and crimp the edges to seal the pie. Cut a few slits in the top crust to allow steam to escape.

6. Egg Wash and Bake:

- In a small bowl, whisk together the egg and milk to create an egg wash. Brush the top crust with the egg wash and sprinkle with sugar.
- Place the pie on a baking sheet to catch any drips and bake in the preheated oven for 45-55 minutes or until the crust is golden brown, and the filling is bubbly.

7. Cool and Serve:

- Allow the pie to cool for at least 2 hours before slicing. Serve with a scoop of vanilla ice cream if desired.

Enjoy your classic apple pie!

Blueberry-Lemon Pie

Ingredients:

For the Pie Crust:

- 1 1/2 cups graham cracker crumbs
- 1/3 cup granulated sugar
- 1/2 cup unsalted butter, melted

For the Blueberry Filling:

- 4 cups fresh or frozen blueberries
- 1 cup granulated sugar
- 1/4 cup cornstarch
- 1/4 teaspoon salt
- 1 tablespoon lemon zest
- 2 tablespoons fresh lemon juice

For the Lemon Cream Topping:

- 1 cup heavy cream
- 1/4 cup powdered sugar
- 1 tablespoon fresh lemon juice
- 1 teaspoon lemon zest

For Garnish:

- Fresh blueberries
- Lemon slices
- Mint leaves

Instructions:

Preheat the Oven:
- Preheat your oven to 350°F (175°C).

Make the Pie Crust:
- In a medium bowl, combine graham cracker crumbs, sugar, and melted butter. Press the mixture into the bottom and up the sides of a 9-inch pie dish. Bake the crust for 8-10 minutes until lightly golden. Allow it to cool completely.

Prepare the Blueberry Filling:
- In a medium saucepan, combine blueberries, sugar, cornstarch, salt, lemon zest, and lemon juice. Cook over medium heat, stirring constantly until the mixture thickens, and the blueberries release their juices (about 8-10 minutes).
- Remove from heat and let it cool to room temperature.

Assemble the Pie:
- Pour the cooled blueberry filling into the prepared pie crust, spreading it evenly.

Make the Lemon Cream Topping:
- In a chilled bowl, whip the heavy cream until it begins to thicken. Add powdered sugar, lemon juice, and lemon zest. Continue whipping until stiff peaks form.

Top the Pie:
- Spread the lemon cream over the blueberry filling, creating decorative peaks with a spatula.

Chill and Garnish:
- Refrigerate the pie for at least 4 hours, allowing it to set. Before serving, garnish with fresh blueberries, lemon slices, and mint leaves.

Serve and Enjoy:
- Slice the pie and serve chilled. Enjoy the delightful combination of sweet blueberries and zesty lemon!

This Blueberry-Lemon Pie is a refreshing and visually appealing dessert that's sure to be a hit at any gathering. Happy baking!

Chocolate Silk Pie

Ingredients:

For the Chocolate Crust:

- 1 1/2 cups chocolate cookie crumbs
- 1/3 cup unsalted butter, melted
- 1/4 cup granulated sugar

For the Chocolate Filling:

- 1 1/2 cups semisweet chocolate chips
- 1/2 cup unsalted butter
- 1 cup granulated sugar
- 1 teaspoon vanilla extract
- 4 large eggs, room temperature

For the Whipped Cream Topping:

- 1 1/2 cups heavy cream
- 1/4 cup powdered sugar
- 1 teaspoon vanilla extract
- Chocolate shavings (for garnish, optional)

Instructions:

Preheat the Oven:
- Preheat your oven to 350°F (175°C).

Make the Chocolate Crust:
- In a medium bowl, combine chocolate cookie crumbs, melted butter, and granulated sugar. Press the mixture into the bottom and up the sides of a 9-inch pie dish. Bake the crust for 8-10 minutes until set. Allow it to cool completely.

Prepare the Chocolate Filling:
- In a heatproof bowl, melt chocolate chips and butter together using a double boiler or in the microwave in short bursts. Stir until smooth and let it cool slightly.

- In a separate bowl, whisk together sugar, vanilla extract, and eggs until well combined. Gradually add the melted chocolate mixture, stirring continuously.

Bake the Filling:
- Pour the chocolate filling into the cooled crust. Bake for 25-30 minutes or until the filling is set around the edges but slightly jiggly in the center. Allow it to cool completely.

Make the Whipped Cream Topping:
- In a chilled bowl, whip the heavy cream until it begins to thicken. Add powdered sugar and vanilla extract. Continue whipping until stiff peaks form.

Top the Pie:
- Spread the whipped cream over the chocolate filling, covering the entire surface. Optionally, garnish with chocolate shavings.

Chill and Serve:
- Refrigerate the pie for at least 4 hours or overnight to allow the flavors to meld and the pie to set. Slice and serve chilled.

Enjoy:
- Indulge in the velvety smooth texture and rich chocolate flavor of this delightful Chocolate Silk Pie!

This Chocolate Silk Pie is a decadent treat that chocolate lovers will surely appreciate. Feel free to adjust the sweetness according to your preference. Happy baking!

Cherry Almond Pie

Ingredients:

For the Pie Crust:

- 1 1/4 cups all-purpose flour
- 1/2 cup unsalted butter, chilled and cubed
- 1/4 cup granulated sugar
- 1/4 teaspoon salt
- 3-4 tablespoons ice water

For the Cherry Filling:

- 4 cups fresh or frozen cherries, pitted
- 1 cup granulated sugar
- 1/4 cup cornstarch
- 1/4 teaspoon almond extract
- 1 tablespoon lemon juice

For the Almond Streusel Topping:

- 1/2 cup all-purpose flour
- 1/3 cup granulated sugar
- 1/3 cup sliced almonds
- 1/4 cup unsalted butter, melted
- 1/4 teaspoon almond extract

Instructions:

Preheat the Oven:
- Preheat your oven to 375°F (190°C).

Make the Pie Crust:
- In a food processor, pulse together flour, sugar, and salt. Add chilled butter and pulse until the mixture resembles coarse crumbs. Gradually add ice water, 1 tablespoon at a time, until the dough comes together.
- Shape the dough into a disk, wrap in plastic wrap, and refrigerate for at least 30 minutes.

Prepare the Cherry Filling:

- In a large bowl, combine pitted cherries, sugar, cornstarch, almond extract, and lemon juice. Toss until the cherries are evenly coated.

Roll Out the Pie Crust:
- On a lightly floured surface, roll out the chilled pie crust into a circle to fit a 9-inch pie dish. Place the crust in the dish and trim any excess. Crimp the edges as desired.

Fill the Pie:
- Pour the prepared cherry filling into the pie crust, spreading it evenly.

Make the Almond Streusel Topping:
- In a bowl, combine flour, sugar, sliced almonds, melted butter, and almond extract. Mix until crumbly.

Top the Pie:
- Sprinkle the almond streusel topping over the cherry filling, covering it evenly.

Bake:
- Place the pie on a baking sheet to catch any drips and bake in the preheated oven for 50-60 minutes or until the crust is golden brown, and the filling is bubbly.

Cool and Serve:
- Allow the pie to cool for at least 2 hours before slicing. Serve at room temperature or slightly warm.

Enjoy:
- Delight in the combination of sweet cherries and the nutty flavor of almond in this Cherry Almond Pie!

Feel free to serve it with a scoop of vanilla ice cream for an extra treat. Enjoy baking!

Pecan Pie

Ingredients:

For the Pie Crust:

- 1 1/4 cups all-purpose flour
- 1/2 cup unsalted butter, chilled and cubed
- 1/4 teaspoon salt
- 3-4 tablespoons ice water

For the Pecan Filling:

- 1 cup granulated sugar
- 1 cup light corn syrup
- 1/3 cup unsalted butter, melted
- 3 large eggs, beaten
- 1 teaspoon vanilla extract
- 2 cups pecan halves

Instructions:

Preheat the Oven:
- Preheat your oven to 350°F (175°C).

Make the Pie Crust:
- In a food processor, pulse together flour and salt. Add chilled butter and pulse until the mixture resembles coarse crumbs. Gradually add ice water, 1 tablespoon at a time, until the dough comes together.
- Shape the dough into a disk, wrap in plastic wrap, and refrigerate for at least 30 minutes.

Roll Out the Pie Crust:
- On a lightly floured surface, roll out the chilled pie crust into a circle to fit a 9-inch pie dish. Place the crust in the dish and trim any excess. Crimp the edges as desired.

Prepare the Pecan Filling:
- In a large bowl, whisk together sugar, corn syrup, melted butter, beaten eggs, and vanilla extract until well combined.
- Stir in the pecan halves, ensuring they are evenly coated in the mixture.

Fill the Pie:
- Pour the pecan filling into the prepared pie crust, spreading the pecans evenly.

Bake:

- Place the pie on a baking sheet to catch any spills and bake in the preheated oven for 50-60 minutes or until the filling is set and the crust is golden brown.

Cool and Serve:
- Allow the pecan pie to cool completely before slicing. The filling will firm up as it cools.

Enjoy:
- Serve slices of Pecan Pie at room temperature or slightly warmed. Optionally, serve with a dollop of whipped cream or a scoop of vanilla ice cream.

Pecan Pie is a classic dessert that's perfect for holidays or any special occasion. Enjoy this sweet and nutty treat!

Banana Cream Pie

Ingredients:

For the Pie Crust:

- 1 1/4 cups graham cracker crumbs
- 1/4 cup granulated sugar
- 1/3 cup unsalted butter, melted

For the Banana Filling:

- 1 cup granulated sugar
- 1/4 cup cornstarch
- 1/4 teaspoon salt
- 2 cups whole milk
- 4 large egg yolks, beaten
- 2 tablespoons unsalted butter
- 1 teaspoon vanilla extract
- 3 ripe bananas, sliced

For the Whipped Cream Topping:

- 1 1/2 cups heavy cream
- 1/4 cup powdered sugar
- 1 teaspoon vanilla extract

For Garnish:

- Sliced bananas
- Chocolate shavings or grated chocolate (optional)

Instructions:

Preheat the Oven:
- Preheat your oven to 350°F (175°C).

Make the Pie Crust:
- In a bowl, combine graham cracker crumbs, sugar, and melted butter. Press the mixture into the bottom and up the sides of a 9-inch pie dish. Bake the crust for 8-10 minutes until set. Allow it to cool completely.

Prepare the Banana Filling:
- In a medium saucepan, whisk together sugar, cornstarch, and salt. Gradually whisk in the milk until smooth. Cook over medium heat, stirring constantly until the mixture thickens and comes to a boil.
- Remove from heat. Gradually whisk about a cup of the hot mixture into the beaten egg yolks. Pour the egg mixture back into the saucepan, stirring continuously.
- Return to heat and cook for an additional 2 minutes, stirring constantly. Remove from heat and stir in butter and vanilla extract. Allow the custard to cool slightly.

Assemble the Pie:
- Arrange sliced bananas over the bottom of the cooled pie crust. Pour the warm banana custard over the bananas, spreading it evenly.

Make the Whipped Cream Topping:
- In a chilled bowl, whip the heavy cream until it begins to thicken. Add powdered sugar and vanilla extract. Continue whipping until stiff peaks form.

Top the Pie:
- Spread the whipped cream over the banana custard, covering the entire surface. Optionally, garnish with sliced bananas and chocolate shavings.

Chill and Serve:
- Refrigerate the banana cream pie for at least 4 hours or until set. Slice and serve chilled.

Enjoy:
- Delight in the creamy banana goodness of this Banana Cream Pie! It's a perfect treat for banana lovers.

This Banana Cream Pie is a classic and comforting dessert that's sure to be a hit. Enjoy baking!

Key Lime Pie

Ingredients:

For the Graham Cracker Crust:

- 1 1/2 cups graham cracker crumbs
- 1/3 cup granulated sugar
- 1/2 cup unsalted butter, melted

For the Key Lime Filling:

- 1 14-ounce can sweetened condensed milk
- 4 large egg yolks
- 1/2 cup key lime juice (freshly squeezed if possible)
- 1 tablespoon key lime zest

For the Whipped Cream Topping:

- 1 cup heavy cream
- 1/4 cup powdered sugar
- 1 teaspoon vanilla extract

For Garnish:

- Key lime slices
- Lime zest

Instructions:

Preheat the Oven:
- Preheat your oven to 350°F (175°C).

Make the Graham Cracker Crust:
- In a bowl, combine graham cracker crumbs, sugar, and melted butter. Press the mixture into the bottom and up the sides of a 9-inch pie dish. Bake the crust for 8-10 minutes until set. Allow it to cool completely.

Prepare the Key Lime Filling:
- In a large bowl, whisk together sweetened condensed milk, egg yolks, key lime juice, and key lime zest until well combined.
- Pour the key lime filling into the cooled graham cracker crust.

Bake the Pie:
- Bake in the preheated oven for 15-20 minutes or until the filling is set and the edges are slightly golden. Allow it to cool to room temperature.

Make the Whipped Cream Topping:
- In a chilled bowl, whip the heavy cream until it begins to thicken. Add powdered sugar and vanilla extract. Continue whipping until stiff peaks form.

Top the Pie:
- Spread the whipped cream over the cooled key lime filling, covering the entire surface.

Chill and Serve:
- Refrigerate the key lime pie for at least 4 hours or until set. The longer it chills, the better the flavors meld.

Garnish and Enjoy:
- Garnish with key lime slices and lime zest just before serving. Slice and enjoy the tangy and refreshing Key Lime Pie!

This Key Lime Pie is a perfect dessert for warm weather or any occasion that calls for a burst of citrusy flavor. Enjoy baking and savoring this delicious treat!

Caramel Apple Crumble Pie

Ingredients:

For the Pie Crust:

- 1 1/4 cups all-purpose flour
- 1/2 cup unsalted butter, chilled and cubed
- 1/4 teaspoon salt
- 3-4 tablespoons ice water

For the Apple Filling:

- 5-6 medium-sized apples, peeled, cored, and sliced (a mix of Granny Smith and Honeycrisp works well)
- 1/2 cup granulated sugar
- 1/4 cup light brown sugar, packed
- 1 teaspoon ground cinnamon
- 1/4 teaspoon ground nutmeg
- 2 tablespoons all-purpose flour
- 1/4 cup caramel sauce (store-bought or homemade)

For the Crumble Topping:

- 1 cup old-fashioned rolled oats
- 1/2 cup all-purpose flour
- 1/2 cup light brown sugar, packed
- 1/4 cup unsalted butter, melted
- 1/2 teaspoon ground cinnamon
- 1/4 cup chopped pecans (optional)

For Drizzling (Optional):

- Additional caramel sauce

Instructions:

Preheat the Oven:
- Preheat your oven to 375°F (190°C).

Make the Pie Crust:

- In a food processor, pulse together flour and salt. Add chilled butter and pulse until the mixture resembles coarse crumbs. Gradually add ice water, 1 tablespoon at a time, until the dough comes together.
- Shape the dough into a disk, wrap in plastic wrap, and refrigerate for at least 30 minutes.

Roll Out the Pie Crust:
- On a lightly floured surface, roll out the chilled pie crust into a circle to fit a 9-inch pie dish. Place the crust in the dish and trim any excess. Crimp the edges as desired.

Prepare the Apple Filling:
- In a large bowl, toss the sliced apples with granulated sugar, brown sugar, cinnamon, nutmeg, and flour until well coated.
- Layer the apple mixture into the pie crust, drizzling caramel sauce over each layer.

Make the Crumble Topping:
- In a bowl, combine oats, flour, brown sugar, melted butter, cinnamon, and chopped pecans. Mix until crumbly.

Top the Pie:
- Sprinkle the crumble topping evenly over the apple filling.

Bake:
- Place the pie on a baking sheet to catch any drips and bake in the preheated oven for 45-50 minutes or until the topping is golden brown, and the apples are tender.

Cool and Drizzle (Optional):
- Allow the pie to cool for at least 2 hours before slicing. If desired, drizzle additional caramel sauce over the top before serving.

Enjoy:
- Serve slices of this Caramel Apple Crumble Pie warm or at room temperature. Enjoy the perfect blend of caramel, spiced apples, and buttery crumble!

This pie is sure to be a crowd-pleaser, especially during the fall season. Happy baking!

Raspberry White Chocolate Pie

Ingredients:

For the Pie Crust:

- 1 1/2 cups chocolate cookie crumbs
- 1/3 cup granulated sugar
- 1/2 cup unsalted butter, melted

For the White Chocolate Filling:

- 8 ounces white chocolate, chopped
- 1 cup heavy cream
- 8 ounces cream cheese, softened
- 1/2 cup powdered sugar
- 1 teaspoon vanilla extract

For the Raspberry Sauce:

- 2 cups fresh or frozen raspberries
- 1/2 cup granulated sugar
- 1 tablespoon cornstarch
- 1 tablespoon lemon juice

For Garnish:

- Fresh raspberries
- White chocolate curls or shavings

Instructions:

Preheat the Oven:
- Preheat your oven to 350°F (175°C).

Make the Pie Crust:
- In a medium bowl, combine chocolate cookie crumbs, sugar, and melted butter. Press the mixture into the bottom and up the sides of a 9-inch pie dish. Bake the crust for 8-10 minutes until set. Allow it to cool completely.

Prepare the White Chocolate Filling:
- In a heatproof bowl, melt the white chocolate over a double boiler or in the microwave in short bursts. Set aside to cool slightly.

- In a separate bowl, whip the heavy cream until stiff peaks form.
- In another bowl, beat the cream cheese until smooth. Add powdered sugar and vanilla extract, beating until well combined.
- Gently fold the melted white chocolate into the cream cheese mixture, followed by the whipped cream, until smooth and well combined.

Fill the Pie Crust:
- Pour the white chocolate filling into the cooled pie crust, spreading it evenly. Refrigerate while preparing the raspberry sauce.

Make the Raspberry Sauce:
- In a saucepan, combine raspberries, sugar, cornstarch, and lemon juice. Cook over medium heat, stirring constantly until the mixture thickens and the raspberries break down (about 5-7 minutes).
- Remove from heat and strain the sauce to remove seeds. Allow it to cool to room temperature.

Top the Pie:
- Pour the raspberry sauce over the white chocolate filling, spreading it evenly.

Chill and Garnish:
- Refrigerate the pie for at least 4 hours or until set. Before serving, garnish with fresh raspberries and white chocolate curls or shavings.

Serve and Enjoy:
- Slice the Raspberry White Chocolate Pie and enjoy the delightful combination of creamy white chocolate and tangy raspberry flavors!

This pie is an elegant and delicious dessert that's perfect for special occasions or whenever you're craving a delightful treat. Enjoy baking!

Coconut Cream Pie

Ingredients:

For the Pie Crust:

- 1 1/4 cups all-purpose flour
- 1/2 cup unsalted butter, chilled and cubed
- 1/4 teaspoon salt
- 3-4 tablespoons ice water

For the Coconut Filling:

- 1 cup sweetened shredded coconut
- 2 cups whole milk
- 1 cup canned coconut milk
- 4 large egg yolks
- 1 cup granulated sugar
- 1/3 cup cornstarch
- 1/4 teaspoon salt
- 1 teaspoon vanilla extract
- 2 tablespoons unsalted butter

For the Whipped Cream Topping:

- 1 1/2 cups heavy cream
- 1/4 cup powdered sugar
- 1 teaspoon vanilla extract

For Garnish:

- Toasted coconut flakes

Instructions:

Preheat the Oven:
- Preheat your oven to 375°F (190°C).

Make the Pie Crust:
- In a food processor, pulse together flour and salt. Add chilled butter and pulse until the mixture resembles coarse crumbs. Gradually add ice water, 1 tablespoon at a time, until the dough comes together.

- In a food processor, pulse together flour and salt. Add chilled butter and pulse until the mixture resembles coarse crumbs. Gradually add ice water, 1 tablespoon at a time, until the dough comes together.
- Shape the dough into a disk, wrap in plastic wrap, and refrigerate for at least 30 minutes.

Roll Out the Pie Crust:
- On a lightly floured surface, roll out the chilled pie crust into a circle to fit a 9-inch pie dish. Place the crust in the dish and trim any excess. Crimp the edges as desired.

Prepare the Apple Filling:
- In a large bowl, toss the sliced apples with granulated sugar, brown sugar, cinnamon, nutmeg, and flour until well coated.
- Layer the apple mixture into the pie crust, drizzling caramel sauce over each layer.

Make the Crumble Topping:
- In a bowl, combine oats, flour, brown sugar, melted butter, cinnamon, and chopped pecans. Mix until crumbly.

Top the Pie:
- Sprinkle the crumble topping evenly over the apple filling.

Bake:
- Place the pie on a baking sheet to catch any drips and bake in the preheated oven for 45-50 minutes or until the topping is golden brown, and the apples are tender.

Cool and Drizzle (Optional):
- Allow the pie to cool for at least 2 hours before slicing. If desired, drizzle additional caramel sauce over the top before serving.

Enjoy:
- Serve slices of this Caramel Apple Crumble Pie warm or at room temperature. Enjoy the perfect blend of caramel, spiced apples, and buttery crumble!

This pie is sure to be a crowd-pleaser, especially during the fall season. Happy baking!

Raspberry White Chocolate Pie

Ingredients:

For the Pie Crust:

- 1 1/2 cups chocolate cookie crumbs
- 1/3 cup granulated sugar
- 1/2 cup unsalted butter, melted

For the White Chocolate Filling:

- 8 ounces white chocolate, chopped
- 1 cup heavy cream
- 8 ounces cream cheese, softened
- 1/2 cup powdered sugar
- 1 teaspoon vanilla extract

For the Raspberry Sauce:

- 2 cups fresh or frozen raspberries
- 1/2 cup granulated sugar
- 1 tablespoon cornstarch
- 1 tablespoon lemon juice

For Garnish:

- Fresh raspberries
- White chocolate curls or shavings

Instructions:

Preheat the Oven:
- Preheat your oven to 350°F (175°C).

Make the Pie Crust:
- In a medium bowl, combine chocolate cookie crumbs, sugar, and melted butter. Press the mixture into the bottom and up the sides of a 9-inch pie dish. Bake the crust for 8-10 minutes until set. Allow it to cool completely.

Prepare the White Chocolate Filling:
- In a heatproof bowl, melt the white chocolate over a double boiler or in the microwave in short bursts. Set aside to cool slightly.

- In a separate bowl, whip the heavy cream until stiff peaks form.
- In another bowl, beat the cream cheese until smooth. Add powdered sugar and vanilla extract, beating until well combined.
- Gently fold the melted white chocolate into the cream cheese mixture, followed by the whipped cream, until smooth and well combined.

Fill the Pie Crust:
- Pour the white chocolate filling into the cooled pie crust, spreading it evenly. Refrigerate while preparing the raspberry sauce.

Make the Raspberry Sauce:
- In a saucepan, combine raspberries, sugar, cornstarch, and lemon juice. Cook over medium heat, stirring constantly until the mixture thickens and the raspberries break down (about 5-7 minutes).
- Remove from heat and strain the sauce to remove seeds. Allow it to cool to room temperature.

Top the Pie:
- Pour the raspberry sauce over the white chocolate filling, spreading it evenly.

Chill and Garnish:
- Refrigerate the pie for at least 4 hours or until set. Before serving, garnish with fresh raspberries and white chocolate curls or shavings.

Serve and Enjoy:
- Slice the Raspberry White Chocolate Pie and enjoy the delightful combination of creamy white chocolate and tangy raspberry flavors!

This pie is an elegant and delicious dessert that's perfect for special occasions or whenever you're craving a delightful treat. Enjoy baking!

Coconut Cream Pie

Ingredients:

For the Pie Crust:

- 1 1/4 cups all-purpose flour
- 1/2 cup unsalted butter, chilled and cubed
- 1/4 teaspoon salt
- 3-4 tablespoons ice water

For the Coconut Filling:

- 1 cup sweetened shredded coconut
- 2 cups whole milk
- 1 cup canned coconut milk
- 4 large egg yolks
- 1 cup granulated sugar
- 1/3 cup cornstarch
- 1/4 teaspoon salt
- 1 teaspoon vanilla extract
- 2 tablespoons unsalted butter

For the Whipped Cream Topping:

- 1 1/2 cups heavy cream
- 1/4 cup powdered sugar
- 1 teaspoon vanilla extract

For Garnish:

- Toasted coconut flakes

Instructions:

Preheat the Oven:
- Preheat your oven to 375°F (190°C).

Make the Pie Crust:
- In a food processor, pulse together flour and salt. Add chilled butter and pulse until the mixture resembles coarse crumbs. Gradually add ice water, 1 tablespoon at a time, until the dough comes together.

- Shape the dough into a disk, wrap in plastic wrap, and refrigerate for at least 30 minutes.

Roll Out the Pie Crust:
- On a lightly floured surface, roll out the chilled pie crust into a circle to fit a 9-inch pie dish. Place the crust in the dish and trim any excess. Crimp the edges as desired.

Toast the Coconut:
- Spread the shredded coconut on a baking sheet and toast in the preheated oven for about 5-7 minutes, or until golden brown. Stir occasionally to ensure even toasting. Set aside.

Prepare the Coconut Filling:
- In a saucepan, combine whole milk, coconut milk, and toasted coconut. Heat over medium heat until it just begins to simmer. Remove from heat and let it steep for about 15-20 minutes.
- In a separate bowl, whisk together egg yolks, sugar, cornstarch, and salt until well combined.
- Gradually whisk the milk mixture into the egg mixture. Return the combined mixture to the saucepan and cook over medium heat, stirring constantly until it thickens.
- Remove from heat and stir in vanilla extract and butter until smooth.

Fill the Pie:
- Pour the coconut filling into the baked and cooled pie crust. Smooth the top with a spatula.

Make the Whipped Cream Topping:
- In a chilled bowl, whip the heavy cream until it begins to thicken. Add powdered sugar and vanilla extract. Continue whipping until stiff peaks form.

Top the Pie:
- Spread the whipped cream over the coconut filling, covering the entire surface.

Garnish:
- Sprinkle toasted coconut flakes over the whipped cream.

Chill and Serve:
- Refrigerate the Coconut Cream Pie for at least 4 hours or until set. Slice and serve chilled.

Enjoy:
- Delight in the creamy coconut goodness of this Coconut Cream Pie!

This pie is a crowd-pleaser with its tropical flavor and silky texture. Enjoy baking and indulging in this classic dessert!

Strawberry Rhubarb Pie

Ingredients:

For the Pie Crust:

- 2 1/2 cups all-purpose flour
- 1 cup unsalted butter, chilled and cubed
- 1 teaspoon salt
- 1 teaspoon granulated sugar
- 6-8 tablespoons ice water

For the Filling:

- 3 cups fresh rhubarb, diced into 1/2-inch pieces
- 3 cups fresh strawberries, hulled and sliced
- 1 cup granulated sugar
- 1/2 cup light brown sugar, packed
- 1/4 cup cornstarch
- 1 teaspoon ground cinnamon
- 1/4 teaspoon salt
- 1 tablespoon lemon juice
- 2 tablespoons unsalted butter, cut into small pieces

For the Egg Wash:

- 1 large egg
- 1 tablespoon water

For Garnish:

- Granulated sugar (for sprinkling)

Instructions:

Make the Pie Crust:
- In a food processor, pulse together flour, salt, and sugar. Add chilled butter and pulse until the mixture resembles coarse crumbs. Gradually add ice water, 1 tablespoon at a time, until the dough comes together.
- Divide the dough into two disks, wrap each in plastic wrap, and refrigerate for at least 1 hour.

Prepare the Filling:
- In a large bowl, combine diced rhubarb, sliced strawberries, granulated sugar, brown sugar, cornstarch, cinnamon, salt, and lemon juice. Toss until the fruits are well coated. Let the mixture sit for about 15 minutes to release some juices.

Preheat the Oven:
- Preheat your oven to 400°F (200°C).

Roll Out the Pie Crust:
- On a lightly floured surface, roll out one of the chilled pie crust disks into a circle to fit a 9-inch pie dish. Transfer the crust to the pie dish.

Fill the Pie:
- Pour the strawberry-rhubarb filling into the prepared pie crust. Dot the top with small pieces of butter.

Roll Out the Top Crust:
- Roll out the second pie crust disk and place it over the filling. Trim and crimp the edges to seal the pie.

Make the Egg Wash:
- In a small bowl, whisk together the egg and water. Brush the top crust with the egg wash.

Vent the Crust:
- Make a few small slits or a decorative pattern in the top crust to allow steam to escape during baking.

Bake:
- Place the pie on a baking sheet to catch any drips and bake in the preheated oven for 45-50 minutes or until the crust is golden brown, and the filling is bubbling.

Cool and Serve:
- Allow the Strawberry Rhubarb Pie to cool for at least 2 hours before slicing. This helps the filling set.

Garnish:
- Optionally, sprinkle the top with granulated sugar for a sweet finish.

Enjoy:
- Slice and serve the Strawberry Rhubarb Pie on its own or with a scoop of vanilla ice cream.

This pie captures the perfect balance of sweet and tart flavors and is a wonderful way to celebrate the flavors of spring and early summer. Enjoy baking and savoring this delicious pie!

Blackberry Galette

Ingredients:

For the Galette Dough:

- 1 1/4 cups all-purpose flour
- 1 tablespoon granulated sugar
- 1/4 teaspoon salt
- 1/2 cup unsalted butter, chilled and cubed
- 3-4 tablespoons ice water

For the Blackberry Filling:

- 3 cups fresh blackberries
- 1/3 cup granulated sugar
- 2 tablespoons cornstarch
- 1 tablespoon lemon juice
- Zest of one lemon

For Assembly:

- 1 tablespoon unsalted butter, melted (for brushing)
- 1-2 tablespoons granulated sugar (for sprinkling)
- Vanilla ice cream or whipped cream (optional, for serving)

Instructions:

Preheat the Oven:
- Preheat your oven to 375°F (190°C).

Make the Galette Dough:
- In a food processor, pulse together flour, sugar, and salt. Add chilled butter and pulse until the mixture resembles coarse crumbs. Gradually add ice water, 1 tablespoon at a time, until the dough comes together.
- Shape the dough into a disk, wrap in plastic wrap, and refrigerate for at least 30 minutes.

Prepare the Blackberry Filling:
- In a bowl, gently toss blackberries with sugar, cornstarch, lemon juice, and lemon zest until the berries are evenly coated.

Roll Out the Dough:

- On a lightly floured surface, roll out the chilled galette dough into a rough circle, about 12 inches in diameter.

Assemble the Galette:
- Transfer the rolled-out dough to a parchment paper-lined baking sheet. Arrange the blackberry filling in the center, leaving a border around the edges.

Fold the Edges:
- Fold the edges of the dough over the berries, creating a rustic and free-form shape. Press gently to seal any cracks in the dough.

Brush with Butter and Sprinkle Sugar:
- Brush the edges of the dough with melted butter and sprinkle with granulated sugar for a golden, slightly crispy crust.

Bake:
- Bake in the preheated oven for 30-35 minutes or until the crust is golden brown, and the blackberries are bubbling.

Cool:
- Allow the Blackberry Galette to cool for about 15 minutes before slicing.

Serve:
- Serve the galette warm or at room temperature. Optionally, top with a scoop of vanilla ice cream or a dollop of whipped cream.

Enjoy:
- Enjoy the simplicity and deliciousness of this Blackberry Galette!

This galette is a perfect way to showcase the natural sweetness of blackberries with minimal fuss. It's a versatile dessert that can be enjoyed any time of the year. Happy baking!

Lemon Meringue Pie

Ingredients:

For the Pie Crust:

- 1 1/4 cups all-purpose flour
- 1/2 cup unsalted butter, chilled and cubed
- 1/4 teaspoon salt
- 3-4 tablespoons ice water

For the Lemon Filling:

- 1 cup granulated sugar
- 1/4 cup cornstarch
- 1/4 teaspoon salt
- 1 1/2 cups water
- 4 large egg yolks, beaten
- 1 tablespoon lemon zest
- 1/2 cup fresh lemon juice
- 2 tablespoons unsalted butter

For the Meringue Topping:

- 4 large egg whites, room temperature
- 1/2 cup granulated sugar
- 1/2 teaspoon cream of tartar
- 1 teaspoon vanilla extract

Instructions:

Make the Pie Crust:
- In a food processor, pulse together flour and salt. Add chilled butter and pulse until the mixture resembles coarse crumbs. Gradually add ice water, 1 tablespoon at a time, until the dough comes together.
- Shape the dough into a disk, wrap in plastic wrap, and refrigerate for at least 30 minutes.

Roll Out the Pie Crust:

- On a lightly floured surface, roll out the chilled pie crust into a circle to fit a 9-inch pie dish. Place the crust in the dish and trim any excess. Crimp the edges as desired. Preheat your oven to 375°F (190°C).

Pre-Bake the Crust:
- Line the pie crust with parchment paper and fill it with pie weights or dried beans. Bake for about 15 minutes. Remove the weights and parchment paper, then bake for an additional 10 minutes or until the crust is golden brown. Allow it to cool.

Prepare the Lemon Filling:
- In a saucepan, whisk together sugar, cornstarch, and salt. Gradually whisk in water until smooth. Cook over medium heat, stirring constantly until the mixture thickens and comes to a boil.
- Remove from heat. Gradually whisk about a cup of the hot mixture into the beaten egg yolks. Pour the egg mixture back into the saucepan, stirring continuously.
- Return to heat and cook for an additional 2 minutes, stirring constantly. Remove from heat and stir in lemon zest, lemon juice, and butter until smooth. Pour the lemon filling into the pre-baked pie crust.

Make the Meringue Topping:
- In a clean, dry bowl, beat the egg whites with an electric mixer until foamy. Add cream of tartar and continue beating. Gradually add sugar, a tablespoon at a time, until stiff peaks form. Add vanilla extract and beat until well combined.

Top the Pie with Meringue:
- Spread the meringue over the hot lemon filling, making sure it touches the crust to prevent shrinking. Create peaks with a spatula for a decorative touch.

Bake the Meringue:
- Bake the pie in the preheated oven for about 12-15 minutes or until the meringue is golden brown.

Cool and Serve:
- Allow the Lemon Meringue Pie to cool completely before slicing. Refrigerate for a few hours to set the filling.

Enjoy:
- Slice and enjoy the tangy and sweet perfection of this classic Lemon Meringue Pie!

This pie is a timeless favorite that's perfect for any occasion. Enjoy baking and savoring this delicious dessert!

Maple Pecan Pumpkin Pie

Ingredients:

For the Pie Crust:

- 1 1/4 cups all-purpose flour
- 1/2 cup unsalted butter, chilled and cubed
- 1/4 teaspoon salt
- 3-4 tablespoons ice water

For the Pecan Layer:

- 1 cup pecan halves
- 1/4 cup pure maple syrup
- 2 tablespoons unsalted butter, melted
- 1 tablespoon all-purpose flour
- Pinch of salt

For the Pumpkin Filling:

- 1 can (15 ounces) pumpkin puree
- 3/4 cup brown sugar, packed
- 2 teaspoons ground cinnamon
- 1/2 teaspoon ground ginger
- 1/4 teaspoon ground cloves
- 1/2 teaspoon salt
- 3 large eggs
- 1 cup heavy cream
- 1/4 cup pure maple syrup
- 1 teaspoon vanilla extract

For Garnish:

- Whipped cream
- Pecan halves
- Maple syrup drizzle

Instructions:

    Make the Pie Crust:

- In a food processor, pulse together flour and salt. Add chilled butter and pulse until the mixture resembles coarse crumbs. Gradually add ice water, 1 tablespoon at a time, until the dough comes together.
- Shape the dough into a disk, wrap in plastic wrap, and refrigerate for at least 30 minutes.

Roll Out the Pie Crust:
- On a lightly floured surface, roll out the chilled pie crust into a circle to fit a 9-inch pie dish. Place the crust in the dish and trim any excess. Crimp the edges as desired. Preheat your oven to 375°F (190°C).

Prepare the Pecan Layer:
- In a bowl, toss pecan halves with maple syrup, melted butter, flour, and a pinch of salt. Spread the pecan mixture over the bottom of the pie crust.

Make the Pumpkin Filling:
- In a large bowl, whisk together pumpkin puree, brown sugar, cinnamon, ginger, cloves, and salt. Add eggs, one at a time, whisking well after each addition.
- Stir in heavy cream, maple syrup, and vanilla extract until smooth. Pour the pumpkin filling over the pecan layer in the pie crust.

Bake:
- Bake in the preheated oven for 45-50 minutes or until the center is set and a toothpick inserted into the center comes out clean.

Cool:
- Allow the pie to cool completely on a wire rack.

Chill:
- For best results, refrigerate the Maple Pecan Pumpkin Pie for a few hours or overnight to allow the flavors to meld.

Garnish and Serve:
- Garnish with whipped cream, pecan halves, and a drizzle of maple syrup just before serving.

Enjoy:
- Slice and enjoy the delicious combination of maple, pecans, and pumpkin in this festive pie!

This Maple Pecan Pumpkin Pie is a delightful addition to holiday gatherings or any time you crave the flavors of fall. Happy baking!

Triple Berry Pie

Ingredients:

For the Pie Crust:

- 2 1/2 cups all-purpose flour
- 1 cup unsalted butter, chilled and cubed
- 1 teaspoon salt
- 1 tablespoon granulated sugar
- 6-8 tablespoons ice water

For the Berry Filling:

- 2 cups fresh strawberries, hulled and halved
- 1 1/2 cups fresh blueberries
- 1 1/2 cups fresh raspberries
- 1 cup granulated sugar
- 1/4 cup cornstarch
- 1 tablespoon lemon juice
- Zest of one lemon

For Assembly:

- 1 tablespoon unsalted butter, cut into small pieces
- 1 large egg (for egg wash)
- 1 tablespoon milk (for egg wash)
- Granulated sugar (for sprinkling)

Instructions:

Make the Pie Crust:
- In a food processor, pulse together flour, salt, and sugar. Add chilled butter and pulse until the mixture resembles coarse crumbs. Gradually add ice water, 1 tablespoon at a time, until the dough comes together.
- Divide the dough into two disks, wrap each in plastic wrap, and refrigerate for at least 1 hour.

Prepare the Berry Filling:

- In a large bowl, gently toss together strawberries, blueberries, raspberries, granulated sugar, cornstarch, lemon juice, and lemon zest until well combined. Set aside.

Preheat the Oven:
- Preheat your oven to 375°F (190°C).

Roll Out the Pie Crust:
- On a lightly floured surface, roll out one of the chilled pie crust disks into a circle to fit a 9-inch pie dish. Place the crust in the dish.

Fill the Pie:
- Pour the mixed berry filling into the prepared pie crust. Dot the top with small pieces of butter.

Roll Out the Top Crust:
- Roll out the second pie crust disk and place it over the filling. Trim and crimp the edges to seal the pie. You can create a lattice crust or a solid crust with slits for steam to escape.

Make the Egg Wash:
- In a small bowl, whisk together the egg and milk to create an egg wash.

Brush with Egg Wash:
- Brush the top crust with the egg wash for a golden finish.

Sprinkle with Sugar:
- Optionally, sprinkle granulated sugar over the top crust for added sweetness and a beautiful sparkle.

Vent the Crust:
- If you've created a solid crust, make a few small slits to allow steam to escape during baking.

Bake:
- Place the pie on a baking sheet to catch any drips and bake in the preheated oven for 45-50 minutes or until the crust is golden brown, and the filling is bubbling.

Cool and Serve:
- Allow the Triple Berry Pie to cool for at least 2 hours before slicing. This helps the filling set.

Enjoy:
- Slice and enjoy the burst of flavors from the trio of strawberries, blueberries, and raspberries in this delicious pie!

This Triple Berry Pie is a wonderful treat, especially during the summer months when berries are at their peak. Enjoy baking and indulging in this delightful dessert!

Chocolate Peanut Butter Pie

Ingredients:

For the Chocolate Cookie Crust:

- 2 cups chocolate cookie crumbs (chocolate graham crackers or chocolate sandwich cookies work well)
- 1/2 cup unsalted butter, melted
- 1/4 cup granulated sugar

For the Peanut Butter Filling:

- 1 cup creamy peanut butter
- 1 package (8 ounces) cream cheese, softened
- 1 cup powdered sugar
- 1 teaspoon vanilla extract

For the Chocolate Ganache Topping:

- 1 cup heavy cream
- 8 ounces semisweet chocolate, chopped
- 2 tablespoons unsalted butter

For Garnish (Optional):

- Chopped peanuts
- Chocolate shavings

Instructions:

Make the Chocolate Cookie Crust:
- In a bowl, combine chocolate cookie crumbs, melted butter, and granulated sugar. Press the mixture into the bottom and up the sides of a 9-inch pie dish. Use the back of a spoon to create an even crust. Chill the crust in the refrigerator while preparing the filling.

Prepare the Peanut Butter Filling:
- In a mixing bowl, beat together creamy peanut butter, softened cream cheese, powdered sugar, and vanilla extract until smooth and well combined.

Fill the Crust:

- Spread the peanut butter filling evenly over the chilled chocolate cookie crust.

Make the Chocolate Ganache Topping:
- In a saucepan, heat the heavy cream until it just begins to simmer. Remove from heat and add the chopped semisweet chocolate and butter. Let it sit for a minute, then stir until smooth and well combined.

Pour the Ganache:
- Pour the chocolate ganache over the peanut butter filling, spreading it to the edges to cover the entire surface.

Chill:
- Place the Chocolate Peanut Butter Pie in the refrigerator and let it chill for at least 4 hours or until set.

Garnish (Optional):
- Before serving, garnish the pie with chopped peanuts and chocolate shavings for added texture and visual appeal.

Slice and Serve:
- Slice the Chocolate Peanut Butter Pie and serve chilled. Enjoy the decadent combination of chocolate and peanut butter in every bite!

This Chocolate Peanut Butter Pie is sure to be a crowd-pleaser, especially for those who love the classic flavor pairing of chocolate and peanut butter. Indulge in the creamy, dreamy goodness of this delightful dessert!

Sweet Potato Pie

Ingredients:

For the Pie Crust:

- 1 1/4 cups all-purpose flour
- 1/2 cup unsalted butter, chilled and cubed
- 1/4 teaspoon salt
- 3-4 tablespoons ice water

For the Sweet Potato Filling:

- 2 cups mashed sweet potatoes (about 2 medium-sized sweet potatoes)
- 1/2 cup unsalted butter, melted
- 1 cup granulated sugar
- 1/2 cup brown sugar, packed
- 1/2 cup evaporated milk
- 2 large eggs, beaten
- 1 teaspoon vanilla extract
- 1/2 teaspoon ground cinnamon
- 1/4 teaspoon ground nutmeg
- 1/4 teaspoon salt

For Garnish (Optional):

- Whipped cream
- Chopped pecans or walnuts
- Ground cinnamon

Instructions:

Make the Pie Crust:
- In a food processor, pulse together flour and salt. Add chilled butter and pulse until the mixture resembles coarse crumbs. Gradually add ice water, 1 tablespoon at a time, until the dough comes together.
- Shape the dough into a disk, wrap in plastic wrap, and refrigerate for at least 30 minutes.

Roll Out the Pie Crust:

- On a lightly floured surface, roll out the chilled pie crust into a circle to fit a 9-inch pie dish. Place the crust in the dish and trim any excess. Crimp the edges as desired.

Preheat the Oven:
- Preheat your oven to 375°F (190°C).

Prepare the Sweet Potato Filling:
- Peel, chop, and boil the sweet potatoes until tender. Mash them until smooth.
- In a large bowl, combine mashed sweet potatoes, melted butter, granulated sugar, brown sugar, evaporated milk, beaten eggs, vanilla extract, cinnamon, nutmeg, and salt. Mix until well combined.

Fill the Pie:
- Pour the sweet potato filling into the prepared pie crust, spreading it evenly.

Bake:
- Bake in the preheated oven for 45-50 minutes or until the center is set and a toothpick inserted into the center comes out clean.

Cool:
- Allow the Sweet Potato Pie to cool completely on a wire rack.

Garnish (Optional):
- Garnish with whipped cream, chopped nuts, and a sprinkle of ground cinnamon just before serving.

Slice and Serve:
- Slice the Sweet Potato Pie and serve at room temperature or chilled. Enjoy the warm and comforting flavors of this classic Southern dessert!

Sweet Potato Pie is a wonderful treat, especially during the fall and Thanksgiving season. The natural sweetness of sweet potatoes combined with warm spices makes it a delightful and comforting dessert. Enjoy baking and savoring this classic pie!

Peach Bourbon Hand Pies

Ingredients:

For the Pie Dough:

- 2 1/2 cups all-purpose flour
- 1 cup unsalted butter, chilled and cubed
- 1 teaspoon salt
- 1 tablespoon granulated sugar
- 6-8 tablespoons ice water

For the Peach Bourbon Filling:

- 3 cups fresh or canned peaches, diced
- 1/2 cup granulated sugar
- 2 tablespoons bourbon
- 1 tablespoon cornstarch
- 1/2 teaspoon ground cinnamon
- 1/4 teaspoon salt
- 1 teaspoon vanilla extract

For Assembly:

- 1 large egg (for egg wash)
- 1 tablespoon water (for egg wash)
- Turbinado sugar (for sprinkling)

Instructions:

Make the Pie Dough:
- In a food processor, pulse together flour, salt, and sugar. Add chilled butter and pulse until the mixture resembles coarse crumbs. Gradually add ice water, 1 tablespoon at a time, until the dough comes together.
- Divide the dough into two disks, wrap each in plastic wrap, and refrigerate for at least 1 hour.

Prepare the Peach Bourbon Filling:
- In a bowl, combine diced peaches, granulated sugar, bourbon, cornstarch, ground cinnamon, salt, and vanilla extract. Mix well and set aside to let the flavors meld.

Preheat the Oven:
- Preheat your oven to 375°F (190°C).

Roll Out the Dough:
- On a lightly floured surface, roll out one of the chilled pie crust disks to about 1/8-inch thickness. Cut out circles (about 4-5 inches in diameter) for the hand pies.

Fill the Hand Pies:
- Place a spoonful of the peach bourbon filling onto one half of each circle, leaving a border around the edges. Fold the other half over the filling, creating a half-moon shape. Press the edges to seal and crimp with a fork.

Make the Egg Wash:
- In a small bowl, whisk together the egg and water to create an egg wash.

Brush with Egg Wash:
- Brush the tops of the hand pies with the egg wash for a golden finish.

Sprinkle with Sugar:
- Sprinkle turbinado sugar over the tops of the hand pies for added sweetness and a beautiful sparkle.

Vent the Pies:
- Use a sharp knife to make a small slit or two on the top of each hand pie to allow steam to escape during baking.

Bake:
- Place the hand pies on a parchment-lined baking sheet and bake in the preheated oven for 18-20 minutes or until the crust is golden brown.

Cool:
- Allow the Peach Bourbon Hand Pies to cool on a wire rack.

Enjoy:
- Serve these delightful hand pies warm or at room temperature. Enjoy the wonderful combination of peach and bourbon flavors in a portable pastry!

Peach Bourbon Hand Pies are a delightful treat, perfect for picnics, brunches, or anytime you crave a handheld dessert. Enjoy baking and savoring these delicious pies!

Oreo Cheesecake Pie

Ingredients:

For the Oreo Crust:

- 2 cups Oreo cookie crumbs (cream removed), about 20-25 cookies
- 1/2 cup unsalted butter, melted

For the Cheesecake Filling:

- 16 ounces (2 blocks) cream cheese, softened
- 1 cup granulated sugar
- 1 teaspoon vanilla extract
- 3 large eggs
- 1 cup sour cream
- 1 cup crushed Oreo cookies (with cream), about 10 cookies

For Garnish (Optional):

- Whipped cream
- Crushed Oreo cookies

Instructions:

Preheat the Oven:
- Preheat your oven to 325°F (163°C).

Make the Oreo Crust:
- In a food processor, pulse the Oreo cookies (cream removed) until fine crumbs. Mix the crumbs with melted butter until well combined. Press the mixture into the bottom of a 9-inch pie dish to form the crust. Chill the crust in the refrigerator while preparing the filling.

Prepare the Cheesecake Filling:
- In a large mixing bowl, beat the softened cream cheese until smooth. Add granulated sugar and vanilla extract, and continue to beat until well combined.
- Add eggs one at a time, beating well after each addition. Stir in sour cream until the mixture is smooth.
- Fold in the crushed Oreo cookies, distributing them evenly throughout the batter.

Fill the Pie Crust:
- Pour the cheesecake filling into the prepared Oreo crust, spreading it evenly.

Bake:
- Bake in the preheated oven for 45-50 minutes or until the center is set and the edges are slightly golden. The center may have a slight jiggle, but it will firm up as it cools.

Cool:
- Allow the Oreo Cheesecake Pie to cool completely on a wire rack.

Chill:
- Once cooled, refrigerate the pie for at least 4 hours or overnight to allow it to set.

Garnish (Optional):
- Before serving, garnish with whipped cream and additional crushed Oreo cookies for a decorative touch.

Slice and Serve:
- Slice the Oreo Cheesecake Pie and serve chilled. Enjoy the rich and creamy goodness of this delightful dessert!

This Oreo Cheesecake Pie is a crowd-pleaser and a perfect treat for Oreo and cheesecake lovers alike. It's an easy-to-make dessert that combines the best of both worlds. Enjoy baking and indulging in this delicious pie!

Cinnamon Roll Apple Pie

Ingredients:

For the Cinnamon Roll Crust:

- 1 package (8 count) refrigerated cinnamon rolls with icing

For the Apple Pie Filling:

- 6 cups peeled and thinly sliced apples (such as Granny Smith or Honeycrisp)
- 1/2 cup granulated sugar
- 1/4 cup brown sugar, packed
- 1 teaspoon ground cinnamon
- 1/4 teaspoon ground nutmeg
- 2 tablespoons all-purpose flour
- 1 tablespoon lemon juice

For the Streusel Topping:

- 1/2 cup all-purpose flour
- 1/4 cup rolled oats
- 1/4 cup brown sugar, packed
- 1/4 cup unsalted butter, cold and cubed

For Glaze:

- Reserved icing from the cinnamon rolls

Instructions:

Preheat the Oven:
- Preheat your oven to 375°F (190°C).

Prepare the Cinnamon Roll Crust:
- Unroll the refrigerated cinnamon rolls and press them into the bottom and up the sides of a 9-inch pie dish, creating a crust. Reserve the icing for later.

Make the Apple Pie Filling:
- In a large bowl, combine the sliced apples, granulated sugar, brown sugar, ground cinnamon, ground nutmeg, all-purpose flour, and lemon juice. Toss until the apples are well coated.

Fill the Cinnamon Roll Crust:
- Fill the cinnamon roll crust with the prepared apple mixture, spreading it evenly.

Prepare the Streusel Topping:
- In a small bowl, combine flour, rolled oats, brown sugar, and cold cubed butter. Use your fingers or a pastry cutter to mix until crumbly.

Top with Streusel:
- Sprinkle the streusel topping over the apple filling, covering it evenly.

Bake:
- Bake in the preheated oven for 40-45 minutes or until the apples are tender, and the streusel is golden brown. If the crust edges start to brown too quickly, you can cover them with aluminum foil.

Cool:
- Allow the Cinnamon Roll Apple Pie to cool on a wire rack.

Prepare the Glaze:
- Microwave the reserved icing from the cinnamon rolls for a few seconds until it's in a pourable consistency.

Drizzle with Glaze:
- Drizzle the glaze over the cooled pie, creating a sweet finishing touch.

Slice and Serve:
- Slice the Cinnamon Roll Apple Pie and serve at room temperature or slightly warmed. Enjoy the delicious combination of cinnamon rolls and apple pie flavors!

This Cinnamon Roll Apple Pie is a unique and tasty twist on the classic apple pie. The cinnamon roll crust adds a comforting sweetness, making it a perfect dessert for any occasion. Enjoy baking and savoring this delightful pie!

S'mores Pie

Ingredients:

For the Graham Cracker Crust:

- 1 1/2 cups graham cracker crumbs
- 1/4 cup granulated sugar
- 1/2 cup unsalted butter, melted

For the Chocolate Filling:

- 1 1/2 cups semisweet chocolate chips
- 3/4 cup heavy cream

For the Marshmallow Topping:

- 2 cups marshmallows (mini marshmallows work well)

For Garnish (Optional):

- Crushed graham crackers
- Chocolate shavings

Instructions:

Preheat the Oven:
- Preheat your oven to 350°F (175°C).

Make the Graham Cracker Crust:
- In a bowl, combine graham cracker crumbs, sugar, and melted butter. Press the mixture into the bottom and up the sides of a 9-inch pie dish. Bake the crust for 8-10 minutes until lightly golden. Allow it to cool.

Prepare the Chocolate Filling:
- In a heatproof bowl, combine semisweet chocolate chips and heavy cream. Melt the chocolate using a double boiler or by microwaving in short intervals, stirring until smooth. Pour the melted chocolate into the cooled graham cracker crust.

Assemble the Pie:
- Spread the chocolate evenly across the crust, creating a smooth chocolate layer.

Add Marshmallow Topping:

- Scatter marshmallows over the chocolate layer, covering the entire surface of the pie.

Broil or Torch the Marshmallows:
- Place the pie under the broiler for a minute or two, or use a kitchen torch to brown the marshmallows until they are golden and toasted. Keep a close eye on them to prevent burning.

Cool:
- Allow the S'mores Pie to cool for a few minutes to set the chocolate and marshmallow topping.

Garnish (Optional):
- Before serving, garnish with crushed graham crackers and chocolate shavings for added texture and visual appeal.

Slice and Serve:
- Slice the S'mores Pie and serve warm or at room temperature. Enjoy the gooey marshmallow, rich chocolate, and graham cracker goodness!

This S'mores Pie is a fantastic way to enjoy the flavors of a classic s'more without needing a campfire. It's a crowd-pleaser and a perfect treat for any occasion. Enjoy making and indulging in this delightful pie!

Espresso Chocolate Pie

Ingredients:

For the Chocolate Cookie Crust:

- 1 1/2 cups chocolate cookie crumbs (chocolate graham crackers or chocolate sandwich cookies work well)
- 1/3 cup unsalted butter, melted
- 1/4 cup granulated sugar

For the Espresso Chocolate Filling:

- 1 1/2 cups semisweet chocolate chips
- 2 tablespoons instant espresso powder
- 1/4 cup hot water
- 1 cup heavy cream
- 1/4 cup unsalted butter, softened
- 1 teaspoon vanilla extract
- Pinch of salt

For Garnish (Optional):

- Whipped cream
- Chocolate shavings
- Espresso beans

Instructions:

Make the Chocolate Cookie Crust:
- In a bowl, combine chocolate cookie crumbs, melted butter, and granulated sugar. Press the mixture into the bottom and up the sides of a 9-inch pie dish. Bake the crust for 8-10 minutes until set. Allow it to cool.

Prepare the Espresso Chocolate Filling:
- In a small bowl, dissolve instant espresso powder in hot water. Set aside to cool slightly.
- In a heatproof bowl, combine semisweet chocolate chips and softened butter.

- In a saucepan, heat the heavy cream until it just begins to simmer. Pour the hot cream over the chocolate and butter. Let it sit for a minute, then stir until smooth and well combined.
- Add the dissolved espresso mixture, vanilla extract, and a pinch of salt to the chocolate mixture. Stir until everything is incorporated.

Fill the Pie Crust:
- Pour the espresso chocolate filling into the cooled chocolate cookie crust, spreading it evenly.

Chill:
- Refrigerate the Espresso Chocolate Pie for at least 4 hours or until set.

Garnish (Optional):
- Before serving, garnish with whipped cream, chocolate shavings, and espresso beans for a decorative touch.

Slice and Serve:
- Slice the Espresso Chocolate Pie and serve chilled. Enjoy the luxurious combination of espresso and chocolate in every bite!

This Espresso Chocolate Pie is a perfect treat for coffee and chocolate lovers. The bold flavor of espresso pairs wonderfully with the richness of the chocolate, creating a sophisticated and indulgent dessert. Enjoy making and savoring this delicious pie!

Fig and Honey Tart

Ingredients:

For the Tart Crust:

- 1 1/2 cups all-purpose flour
- 1/2 cup unsalted butter, chilled and cubed
- 1/4 cup granulated sugar
- 1/4 teaspoon salt
- 1 large egg yolk
- 2 tablespoons ice water

For the Honey-Almond Filling:

- 1 cup almond flour
- 1/3 cup granulated sugar
- 1/4 cup unsalted butter, softened
- 2 tablespoons honey
- 1 large egg
- 1 teaspoon vanilla extract
- 1/4 teaspoon almond extract (optional)
- Pinch of salt

For Topping:

- Fresh figs, halved or quartered, depending on size
- Honey, for drizzling
- Chopped pistachios or almonds for garnish (optional)

Instructions:

Make the Tart Crust:
- In a food processor, pulse together flour, sugar, and salt. Add chilled butter and pulse until the mixture resembles coarse crumbs. Add the egg yolk and ice water, pulsing until the dough comes together.
- Shape the dough into a disk, wrap in plastic wrap, and refrigerate for at least 30 minutes.

Roll Out the Tart Crust:

- On a lightly floured surface, roll out the chilled tart dough into a circle to fit a tart pan. Press the dough into the pan, trimming any excess. Prick the bottom with a fork and refrigerate for another 15 minutes.

Preheat the Oven:

- Preheat your oven to 375°F (190°C).

Prepare the Honey-Almond Filling:

- In a bowl, combine almond flour, sugar, softened butter, honey, egg, vanilla extract, almond extract (if using), and a pinch of salt. Mix until smooth and well combined.

Fill the Tart Crust:

- Spread the honey-almond filling evenly over the chilled tart crust.

Arrange the Figs:

- Arrange the fresh fig halves or quarters on top of the almond filling in an attractive pattern.

Bake:

- Bake the Fig and Honey Tart in the preheated oven for 25-30 minutes or until the crust is golden and the filling is set.

Cool:

- Allow the tart to cool completely on a wire rack.

Drizzle with Honey:

- Before serving, drizzle honey over the top of the figs for a sweet finish.

Garnish (Optional):

- Optionally, garnish with chopped pistachios or almonds for added texture.

Slice and Serve:

- Slice the Fig and Honey Tart and serve at room temperature. Enjoy the combination of sweet figs, almond filling, and honey in this elegant dessert!

This Fig and Honey Tart is a beautiful and sophisticated dessert that's perfect for special occasions or whenever you want to indulge in the natural sweetness of fresh figs. Enjoy making and savoring this delightful tart!

Caramel Pecan Chocolate Pie

Ingredients:

For the Chocolate Cookie Crust:

- 1 1/2 cups chocolate cookie crumbs (chocolate graham crackers or chocolate sandwich cookies work well)
- 1/3 cup unsalted butter, melted
- 1/4 cup granulated sugar

For the Pecan Caramel Layer:

- 1 cup chopped pecans
- 1/2 cup unsalted butter
- 1 cup brown sugar, packed
- 1/2 cup heavy cream
- 1 teaspoon vanilla extract
- Pinch of salt

For the Chocolate Ganache:

- 1 cup semisweet chocolate chips
- 1/2 cup heavy cream

For Garnish:

- Chopped pecans
- Sea salt flakes (optional)

Instructions:

Make the Chocolate Cookie Crust:
- In a bowl, combine chocolate cookie crumbs, melted butter, and granulated sugar. Press the mixture into the bottom and up the sides of a 9-inch pie dish. Bake the crust for 8-10 minutes until set. Allow it to cool.

Prepare the Pecan Caramel Layer:
- In a saucepan over medium heat, melt butter. Add chopped pecans and toast them for a few minutes until fragrant.

- Stir in brown sugar, heavy cream, vanilla extract, and a pinch of salt. Bring the mixture to a gentle boil, stirring constantly. Let it simmer for 2-3 minutes until it thickens slightly.
- Pour the pecan caramel mixture over the cooled chocolate cookie crust. Spread it evenly.

Make the Chocolate Ganache:
- In a heatproof bowl, combine semisweet chocolate chips and heavy cream. Melt the chocolate using a double boiler or by microwaving in short intervals, stirring until smooth.
- Pour the chocolate ganache over the pecan caramel layer, spreading it evenly.

Chill:
- Refrigerate the Caramel Pecan Chocolate Pie for at least 4 hours or until the layers are set.

Garnish:
- Before serving, garnish with chopped pecans and a sprinkle of sea salt flakes if desired.

Slice and Serve:
- Slice the Caramel Pecan Chocolate Pie and serve chilled. Enjoy the decadent layers of caramel, pecans, and chocolate in every bite!

This Caramel Pecan Chocolate Pie is a perfect treat for those who love the combination of sweet caramel, crunchy pecans, and rich chocolate. It's a show-stopping dessert for any occasion. Enjoy making and indulging in this delightful pie!

Lemon Blueberry Chess Pie

Ingredients:

For the Pie Crust:

- 1 1/4 cups all-purpose flour
- 1/2 cup unsalted butter, chilled and cubed
- 1/4 teaspoon salt
- 3-4 tablespoons ice water

For the Lemon Blueberry Filling:

- 1 cup granulated sugar
- 1/2 cup unsalted butter, melted and cooled
- 3 large eggs
- 1 tablespoon cornmeal
- 1 tablespoon all-purpose flour
- 1 tablespoon lemon zest
- 1/4 cup fresh lemon juice
- 1 cup fresh blueberries

For Garnish:

- Powdered sugar (for dusting)
- Additional blueberries and lemon slices (optional)

Instructions:

Make the Pie Crust:
- In a food processor, pulse together flour and salt. Add chilled butter and pulse until the mixture resembles coarse crumbs. Gradually add ice water, 1 tablespoon at a time, until the dough comes together.
- Shape the dough into a disk, wrap in plastic wrap, and refrigerate for at least 30 minutes.

Roll Out the Pie Crust:
- On a lightly floured surface, roll out the chilled pie crust into a circle to fit a 9-inch pie dish. Place the crust in the dish and trim any excess. Crimp the edges as desired.

Preheat the Oven:

- Preheat your oven to 350°F (175°C).

Prepare the Lemon Blueberry Filling:
- In a large bowl, whisk together sugar, melted butter, eggs, cornmeal, flour, lemon zest, and lemon juice until well combined.
- Gently fold in fresh blueberries.

Fill the Pie Crust:
- Pour the lemon blueberry filling into the prepared pie crust, spreading it evenly.

Bake:
- Bake in the preheated oven for 45-50 minutes or until the center is set and the top is golden brown. If the crust edges start to brown too quickly, you can cover them with aluminum foil.

Cool:
- Allow the Lemon Blueberry Chess Pie to cool completely on a wire rack.

Garnish:
- Before serving, dust the top with powdered sugar. Garnish with additional blueberries and lemon slices if desired.

Slice and Serve:
- Slice the Lemon Blueberry Chess Pie and serve at room temperature. Enjoy the delightful combination of tangy lemon and sweet blueberries in this unique chess pie!

This Lemon Blueberry Chess Pie is a refreshing and flavorful dessert that's perfect for spring and summer. The chess pie's creamy texture combined with the burst of blueberries and zesty lemon creates a delightful treat. Enjoy making and savoring this delicious pie!

Raspberry Chocolate Ganache Tart

Ingredients:

For the Chocolate Tart Shell:

- 1 1/4 cups all-purpose flour
- 1/4 cup unsweetened cocoa powder
- 1/2 cup unsalted butter, cold and cubed
- 1/4 cup granulated sugar
- 1/4 teaspoon salt
- 1 large egg yolk
- 2 tablespoons ice water

For the Chocolate Ganache:

- 8 ounces semisweet chocolate, finely chopped
- 1 cup heavy cream
- 2 tablespoons unsalted butter
- 1 teaspoon vanilla extract

For Topping:

- Fresh raspberries
- Powdered sugar (for dusting)

Instructions:

Make the Chocolate Tart Shell:
- In a food processor, combine flour, cocoa powder, cold butter, sugar, and salt. Pulse until the mixture resembles coarse crumbs.
- Add the egg yolk and ice water. Pulse until the dough comes together. Shape the dough into a disk, wrap in plastic wrap, and refrigerate for at least 30 minutes.

Roll Out the Tart Shell:
- On a lightly floured surface, roll out the chilled chocolate tart dough into a circle to fit a 9-inch tart pan. Press the dough into the pan, trimming any excess. Prick the bottom with a fork and refrigerate for another 15 minutes.

Preheat the Oven:

- Preheat your oven to 350°F (175°C).

Bake the Tart Shell:
- Bake the chocolate tart shell in the preheated oven for 15-18 minutes or until it's set. Allow it to cool completely.

Prepare the Chocolate Ganache:
- Place finely chopped chocolate in a heatproof bowl. In a saucepan, heat the heavy cream and butter over medium heat until it just begins to simmer.
- Pour the hot cream mixture over the chocolate. Let it sit for a minute, then stir until smooth and glossy. Add vanilla extract and stir until well combined.

Fill the Tart Shell with Ganache:
- Pour the chocolate ganache into the cooled chocolate tart shell, spreading it evenly.

Chill:
- Refrigerate the tart for at least 2 hours or until the ganache is set.

Top with Raspberries:
- Before serving, arrange fresh raspberries on top of the chocolate ganache.

Dust with Powdered Sugar:
- Just before serving, dust the top with powdered sugar for a decorative touch.

Slice and Serve:
- Slice the Raspberry Chocolate Ganache Tart and serve chilled. Enjoy the luxurious combination of rich chocolate and the burst of raspberry flavor!

This Raspberry Chocolate Ganache Tart is a show-stopping dessert that's perfect for special occasions or when you want to impress with a decadent treat. The smooth chocolate ganache paired with the tartness of fresh raspberries creates a delightful flavor balance. Enjoy making and savoring this delicious tart!

Buttermilk Pie

Ingredients:

For the Pie Crust:

- 1 1/4 cups all-purpose flour
- 1/2 cup unsalted butter, chilled and cubed
- 1/4 teaspoon salt
- 2-3 tablespoons ice water

For the Buttermilk Filling:

- 1 1/2 cups granulated sugar
- 1/4 cup all-purpose flour
- 1/2 cup unsalted butter, melted and cooled
- 3 large eggs
- 1 cup buttermilk
- 1 teaspoon vanilla extract
- 1 tablespoon lemon juice (optional)
- Zest of 1 lemon (optional)
- Pinch of salt

Instructions:

Make the Pie Crust:
- In a food processor, pulse together flour and salt. Add chilled butter and pulse until the mixture resembles coarse crumbs. Gradually add ice water, 1 tablespoon at a time, until the dough comes together.
- Shape the dough into a disk, wrap in plastic wrap, and refrigerate for at least 30 minutes.

Roll Out the Pie Crust:
- On a lightly floured surface, roll out the chilled pie crust into a circle to fit a 9-inch pie dish. Place the crust in the dish, trimming any excess. Crimp the edges as desired.

Preheat the Oven:
- Preheat your oven to 350°F (175°C).

Prepare the Buttermilk Filling:

- In a large bowl, whisk together sugar, flour, melted butter, eggs, buttermilk, vanilla extract, lemon juice (if using), lemon zest (if using), and a pinch of salt until well combined.

Fill the Pie Crust:
- Pour the buttermilk filling into the prepared pie crust, spreading it evenly.

Bake:
- Bake in the preheated oven for 45-50 minutes or until the center is set and the top is golden brown. If the crust edges start to brown too quickly, you can cover them with aluminum foil.

Cool:
- Allow the Buttermilk Pie to cool completely on a wire rack.

Slice and Serve:
- Slice the Buttermilk Pie and serve at room temperature or chilled. Enjoy the creamy, custard-like texture and the delightful flavor of buttermilk!

Buttermilk Pie is a Southern classic that's simple to make and always a crowd-pleaser. It's a perfect dessert for any occasion, and its smooth filling is sure to be a hit with friends and family. Enjoy making and savoring this delicious Buttermilk Pie!

Apple Cranberry Walnut Tart

Ingredients:

For the Tart Crust:

- 1 1/4 cups all-purpose flour
- 1/4 cup granulated sugar
- 1/2 cup unsalted butter, chilled and cubed
- 1 large egg yolk
- 2 tablespoons ice water

For the Filling:

- 3 large apples, peeled, cored, and thinly sliced (such as Granny Smith or Honeycrisp)
- 1/2 cup dried cranberries
- 1/2 cup chopped walnuts
- 1/4 cup granulated sugar
- 2 tablespoons brown sugar
- 1 teaspoon ground cinnamon
- 1/4 teaspoon ground nutmeg
- 1 tablespoon lemon juice

For the Streusel Topping:

- 1/2 cup all-purpose flour
- 1/4 cup granulated sugar
- 1/4 cup cold unsalted butter, cubed

For Garnish:

- Powdered sugar (for dusting)
- Vanilla ice cream (optional)

Instructions:

Make the Tart Crust:
- In a food processor, pulse together flour and sugar. Add chilled butter and pulse until the mixture resembles coarse crumbs. Add egg yolk and ice water, pulsing until the dough comes together.

- Shape the dough into a disk, wrap in plastic wrap, and refrigerate for at least 30 minutes.

Roll Out the Tart Crust:
- On a lightly floured surface, roll out the chilled tart dough into a circle to fit a 9-inch tart pan. Press the dough into the pan, trimming any excess. Prick the bottom with a fork and refrigerate for another 15 minutes.

Preheat the Oven:
- Preheat your oven to 375°F (190°C).

Prepare the Filling:
- In a large bowl, combine sliced apples, dried cranberries, chopped walnuts, granulated sugar, brown sugar, cinnamon, nutmeg, and lemon juice. Toss until the ingredients are well combined.

Fill the Tart Shell:
- Arrange the apple-cranberry-walnut filling in the chilled tart shell, spreading it evenly.

Make the Streusel Topping:
- In a small bowl, combine flour, granulated sugar, and cold cubed butter. Use your fingers or a pastry cutter to mix until crumbly. Sprinkle the streusel over the filling.

Bake:
- Bake the Apple Cranberry Walnut Tart in the preheated oven for 35-40 minutes or until the crust is golden and the filling is bubbling.

Cool:
- Allow the tart to cool on a wire rack.

Dust with Powdered Sugar:
- Before serving, dust the top with powdered sugar for a decorative touch.

Serve:
- Slice the Apple Cranberry Walnut Tart and serve at room temperature or slightly warmed. Optionally, serve with a scoop of vanilla ice cream for an extra treat.

This Apple Cranberry Walnut Tart is a wonderful fall dessert, and the combination of flavors and textures makes it a delightful treat for any occasion. Enjoy making and savoring this delicious tart!

Bourbon Chocolate Pecan Pie

Ingredients:

For the Pie Crust:

- 1 1/4 cups all-purpose flour
- 1/2 cup unsalted butter, chilled and cubed
- 1/4 teaspoon salt
- 2 tablespoons granulated sugar
- 3-4 tablespoons ice water

For the Filling:

- 3 large eggs
- 1 cup granulated sugar
- 1 cup light corn syrup
- 1/4 cup unsalted butter, melted and cooled
- 2 tablespoons bourbon
- 1 teaspoon vanilla extract
- 1/4 teaspoon salt
- 1 1/2 cups pecan halves
- 1 cup semisweet chocolate chips or chopped chocolate

Instructions:

Make the Pie Crust:
- In a food processor, pulse together flour, sugar, and salt. Add chilled butter and pulse until the mixture resembles coarse crumbs. Gradually add ice water, 1 tablespoon at a time, until the dough comes together.
- Shape the dough into a disk, wrap in plastic wrap, and refrigerate for at least 30 minutes.

Roll Out the Pie Crust:
- On a lightly floured surface, roll out the chilled pie crust into a circle to fit a 9-inch pie dish. Press the dough into the pan, trimming any excess. Crimp the edges as desired.

Preheat the Oven:
- Preheat your oven to 350°F (175°C).

Prepare the Filling:

- In a bowl, whisk together eggs, granulated sugar, corn syrup, melted butter, bourbon, vanilla extract, and salt until well combined.
- Stir in pecan halves and chocolate chips.

Fill the Pie Crust:
- Pour the pecan and chocolate filling into the prepared pie crust, spreading it evenly.

Bake:
- Bake in the preheated oven for 50-55 minutes or until the center is set and the top is golden brown. If the crust edges start to brown too quickly, you can cover them with aluminum foil.

Cool:
- Allow the Bourbon Chocolate Pecan Pie to cool completely on a wire rack.

Chill (Optional):
- For optimal flavor, you can chill the pie in the refrigerator for a few hours before serving.

Slice and Serve:
- Slice the Bourbon Chocolate Pecan Pie and serve at room temperature or slightly chilled. Enjoy the decadent combination of bourbon, chocolate, and pecans!

This Bourbon Chocolate Pecan Pie is a delightful treat for bourbon and chocolate lovers. The addition of bourbon adds depth to the traditional pecan pie, making it a perfect dessert for special occasions or holiday celebrations. Enjoy making and savoring this delicious pie!

Caramel Banana Cream Pie

Ingredients:

For the Pie Crust:

- 1 1/4 cups graham cracker crumbs
- 1/4 cup granulated sugar
- 1/2 cup unsalted butter, melted

For the Caramel Sauce:

- 1 cup granulated sugar
- 1/4 cup water
- 1/2 cup heavy cream
- 2 tablespoons unsalted butter
- 1 teaspoon vanilla extract
- Pinch of salt

For the Banana Filling:

- 3 large bananas, ripe but firm, sliced
- 1 tablespoon lemon juice (to prevent browning)

For the Cream Filling:

- 1/2 cup granulated sugar
- 1/4 cup cornstarch
- 1/4 teaspoon salt
- 2 cups whole milk
- 4 large egg yolks, beaten
- 2 tablespoons unsalted butter
- 1 teaspoon vanilla extract

For Whipped Cream Topping:

- 1 cup heavy cream
- 2 tablespoons powdered sugar
- 1/2 teaspoon vanilla extract

Instructions:

Make the Pie Crust:
- In a bowl, combine graham cracker crumbs, sugar, and melted butter. Press the mixture into the bottom and up the sides of a 9-inch pie dish. Bake the crust for 8-10 minutes until lightly golden. Allow it to cool.

Prepare the Caramel Sauce:
- In a saucepan, combine sugar and water over medium heat. Stir until the sugar dissolves, then let it cook without stirring until it reaches a deep amber color.
- Remove the saucepan from heat and carefully add the heavy cream, butter, vanilla extract, and a pinch of salt. Stir until smooth. Let the caramel sauce cool to room temperature.

Make the Banana Filling:
- Slice the bananas and toss them with lemon juice to prevent browning. Arrange the banana slices in the cooled pie crust.

Prepare the Cream Filling:
- In a saucepan, whisk together sugar, cornstarch, salt, and milk over medium heat. Cook, stirring constantly, until the mixture thickens.
- Temper the beaten egg yolks by gradually whisking in some of the hot milk mixture. Then, whisk the tempered yolks back into the saucepan.
- Continue cooking and stirring until the mixture reaches a pudding-like consistency. Remove from heat and stir in butter and vanilla extract. Let it cool slightly.

Assemble the Pie:
- Pour the cream filling over the banana slices in the pie crust.

Drizzle with Caramel:
- Drizzle the cooled caramel sauce over the banana cream filling, reserving some for garnish.

Chill:
- Refrigerate the pie for at least 4 hours or until set.

Make Whipped Cream Topping:
- In a chilled bowl, whip the heavy cream until it begins to thicken. Add powdered sugar and vanilla extract. Continue whipping until stiff peaks form.

Top and Garnish:
- Spread the whipped cream over the chilled pie. Drizzle with additional caramel sauce.

Serve and Enjoy:

- Slice the Caramel Banana Cream Pie and serve chilled. Enjoy the delightful combination of creamy filling, sweet bananas, and rich caramel!

This Caramel Banana Cream Pie is a luscious and indulgent dessert that's sure to satisfy your sweet cravings. The caramel adds a luxurious touch to the classic banana cream pie. Enjoy making and savoring this delicious pie!

Pear and Gorgonzola Galette

Ingredients:

For the Galette Dough:

- 1 1/4 cups all-purpose flour
- 1/4 teaspoon salt
- 1/2 cup unsalted butter, chilled and cubed
- 2 tablespoons granulated sugar
- 3-4 tablespoons ice water

For the Filling:

- 3 ripe pears, peeled, cored, and thinly sliced
- 1/2 cup crumbled Gorgonzola cheese
- 2 tablespoons honey
- 1 tablespoon balsamic glaze (optional)
- 1 tablespoon chopped fresh thyme leaves
- 1 tablespoon granulated sugar (for sprinkling)

For Egg Wash:

- 1 egg, beaten

Instructions:

Make the Galette Dough:
- In a food processor, pulse together flour, salt, and sugar. Add chilled butter and pulse until the mixture resembles coarse crumbs.
- Gradually add ice water, 1 tablespoon at a time, pulsing until the dough just comes together.
- Shape the dough into a disk, wrap in plastic wrap, and refrigerate for at least 30 minutes.

Preheat the Oven:
- Preheat your oven to 375°F (190°C).

Roll Out the Galette Dough:
- On a lightly floured surface, roll out the chilled galette dough into a circle about 12 inches in diameter. Transfer the rolled-out dough to a parchment paper-lined baking sheet.

Prepare the Filling:
- Arrange the pear slices in the center of the rolled-out dough, leaving a border around the edges.
- Sprinkle crumbled Gorgonzola over the pear slices. Drizzle honey and balsamic glaze (if using) over the pears and cheese. Sprinkle chopped thyme over the filling.

Fold and Seal:
- Fold the edges of the galette dough over the filling, creating a rustic, free-form shape. Press gently to seal the edges.

Brush with Egg Wash:
- Brush the edges of the galette with beaten egg. Sprinkle granulated sugar over the edges for a golden finish.

Bake:
- Bake in the preheated oven for 30-35 minutes or until the crust is golden brown and the pears are tender.

Cool:
- Allow the Pear and Gorgonzola Galette to cool on the baking sheet for a few minutes before transferring it to a wire rack.

Serve:
- Serve the galette warm or at room temperature. Optionally, drizzle with additional honey or balsamic glaze before serving.

Enjoy:
- Slice and enjoy the delightful combination of sweet pears, savory Gorgonzola, and aromatic thyme in this rustic galette!

This Pear and Gorgonzola Galette is a versatile and elegant dish that works well as a savory appetizer or a delicious dessert. The combination of flavors creates a balance that's sure to impress your taste buds. Enjoy making and savoring this delightful galette!

Chocolate Mint Grasshopper Pie

Ingredients:

For the Chocolate Cookie Crust:

- 2 cups chocolate cookie crumbs (you can use chocolate sandwich cookies with the filling removed)
- 1/2 cup unsalted butter, melted

For the Chocolate Mint Filling:

- 1 1/2 cups chocolate chips (dark or semisweet)
- 1/3 cup unsalted butter
- 1 teaspoon vanilla extract
- 1/2 teaspoon peppermint extract
- Green food coloring (optional)
- 2 cups heavy cream
- 1/4 cup powdered sugar

For Garnish:

- Whipped cream
- Chocolate shavings or curls
- Fresh mint leaves

Instructions:

Make the Chocolate Cookie Crust:
- In a bowl, combine chocolate cookie crumbs and melted butter. Press the mixture into the bottom and up the sides of a 9-inch pie dish to form the crust. Place it in the refrigerator to set while you prepare the filling.

Prepare the Chocolate Mint Filling:
- In a heatproof bowl, melt chocolate chips and butter together. You can use a double boiler or microwave in short bursts, stirring between each burst.
- Once melted, stir in vanilla extract, peppermint extract, and green food coloring if desired. Let the mixture cool to room temperature.

Whip the Cream:
- In a separate bowl, whip the heavy cream and powdered sugar until stiff peaks form.

Combine Filling and Whipped Cream:
- Gently fold the cooled chocolate mint mixture into the whipped cream until well combined. Be careful not to deflate the whipped cream.

Fill the Pie Crust:
- Pour the chocolate mint filling into the prepared chocolate cookie crust, spreading it evenly.

Chill:
- Refrigerate the Grasshopper Pie for at least 4 hours or until set.

Garnish:
- Before serving, garnish the pie with a dollop of whipped cream, chocolate shavings or curls, and fresh mint leaves.

Slice and Serve:
- Slice the Chocolate Mint Grasshopper Pie and serve chilled. Enjoy the decadent combination of chocolate and mint in every bite!

This Chocolate Mint Grasshopper Pie is a refreshing and indulgent dessert, perfect for mint chocolate lovers. The creamy filling and chocolate cookie crust create a delightful texture, while the minty flavor adds a cool and refreshing touch. Enjoy making and savoring this delicious pie!

Strawberry Basil Mascarpone Tart

Ingredients:

For the Tart Crust:

- 1 1/4 cups all-purpose flour
- 1/4 cup granulated sugar
- 1/2 cup unsalted butter, chilled and cubed
- 1/4 teaspoon salt
- 1 large egg yolk
- 2 tablespoons ice water

For the Mascarpone Filling:

- 8 ounces mascarpone cheese, softened
- 1/2 cup powdered sugar
- 1 teaspoon vanilla extract
- Zest of 1 lemon

For the Strawberry Basil Topping:

- 2 cups fresh strawberries, hulled and sliced
- 1/4 cup granulated sugar
- 2 tablespoons balsamic glaze
- Fresh basil leaves for garnish

Instructions:

Make the Tart Crust:
- In a food processor, pulse together flour, sugar, and salt. Add chilled butter and pulse until the mixture resembles coarse crumbs. Add egg yolk and ice water, pulsing until the dough comes together.
- Shape the dough into a disk, wrap in plastic wrap, and refrigerate for at least 30 minutes.

Roll Out the Tart Crust:
- On a lightly floured surface, roll out the chilled tart dough into a circle to fit a 9-inch tart pan. Press the dough into the pan, trimming any excess. Prick the bottom with a fork and refrigerate for another 15 minutes.

Preheat the Oven:

- Preheat your oven to 375°F (190°C).

Bake the Tart Crust:
- Bake the tart crust in the preheated oven for 15-18 minutes or until it's set and lightly golden. Allow it to cool completely.

Prepare the Mascarpone Filling:
- In a bowl, whisk together mascarpone cheese, powdered sugar, vanilla extract, and lemon zest until smooth and well combined.

Fill the Tart:
- Spread the mascarpone filling evenly over the cooled tart crust.

Prepare the Strawberry Basil Topping:
- In a bowl, combine sliced strawberries, granulated sugar, and balsamic glaze. Toss until the strawberries are coated.

Top the Tart:
- Arrange the strawberry mixture over the mascarpone filling, ensuring an even distribution.

Chill:
- Refrigerate the Strawberry Basil Mascarpone Tart for at least 1-2 hours to allow the flavors to meld.

Garnish and Serve:
- Before serving, garnish the tart with fresh basil leaves. Slice and serve chilled.

This Strawberry Basil Mascarpone Tart offers a delightful blend of flavors and textures, making it a perfect treat for spring and summer. The sweetness of strawberries, the creamy mascarpone, and the hint of basil create a harmonious and refreshing dessert. Enjoy making and savoring this delicious tart!

Coconut Lime Icebox Pie

Ingredients:

For the Crust:

- 2 cups graham cracker crumbs
- 1/2 cup unsalted butter, melted
- 1/4 cup granulated sugar

For the Filling:

- 1 can (14 ounces) sweetened condensed milk
- 1 cup coconut cream
- 1/2 cup coconut milk
- 1/2 cup fresh lime juice
- Zest of 2 limes
- 1 teaspoon vanilla extract

For the Whipped Cream Topping:

- 1 cup heavy cream
- 2 tablespoons powdered sugar
- Shredded coconut and lime zest for garnish

Instructions:

Make the Crust:
- In a bowl, combine graham cracker crumbs, melted butter, and granulated sugar. Press the mixture into the bottom and up the sides of a 9-inch pie dish to form the crust. Place it in the refrigerator to set while you prepare the filling.

Prepare the Filling:
- In a large bowl, whisk together sweetened condensed milk, coconut cream, coconut milk, lime juice, lime zest, and vanilla extract until well combined.

Fill the Crust:
- Pour the coconut lime filling into the prepared graham cracker crust, spreading it evenly.

Chill:

- Refrigerate the pie for at least 4 hours or overnight to allow it to set.

Make the Whipped Cream Topping:
- In a chilled bowl, whip the heavy cream and powdered sugar until stiff peaks form.

Top the Pie:
- Spread the whipped cream over the chilled pie, creating decorative peaks with a spatula.

Garnish:
- Garnish the Coconut Lime Icebox Pie with shredded coconut and additional lime zest.

Slice and Serve:
- Slice the pie and serve chilled. Enjoy the tropical and citrusy flavors of coconut and lime!

This Coconut Lime Icebox Pie is a perfect dessert for warm days, and its no-bake nature makes it simple to prepare. The combination of coconut, lime, and the creamy filling creates a delicious and satisfying treat. Enjoy making and savoring this delightful pie!

Cinnamon Apple Crustless Pie

Ingredients:

For the Apple Filling:

- 5-6 medium-sized apples, peeled, cored, and thinly sliced (a mix of sweet and tart varieties like Honeycrisp and Granny Smith works well)
- 1/2 cup granulated sugar
- 1 teaspoon ground cinnamon
- 1/4 teaspoon ground nutmeg
- 1 tablespoon lemon juice

For the Custard:

- 3 large eggs
- 1 cup whole milk
- 1/2 cup heavy cream
- 1/2 cup granulated sugar
- 1 teaspoon vanilla extract

For Topping:

- 2 tablespoons unsalted butter, melted
- 1 tablespoon granulated sugar
- 1/2 teaspoon ground cinnamon

Instructions:

Preheat the Oven:
- Preheat your oven to 350°F (175°C). Grease a 9-inch pie dish.

Prepare the Apple Filling:
- In a large bowl, combine sliced apples, granulated sugar, ground cinnamon, ground nutmeg, and lemon juice. Toss until the apples are well coated in the sugar and spices.

Arrange Apples in Pie Dish:
- Spread the coated apple slices evenly in the greased pie dish.

Make the Custard:
- In a separate bowl, whisk together eggs, whole milk, heavy cream, granulated sugar, and vanilla extract until well combined.

Pour Custard Over Apples:
- Pour the custard mixture evenly over the arranged apple slices in the pie dish.

Bake:
- Bake in the preheated oven for 40-45 minutes or until the custard is set and the top is golden brown.

Prepare the Topping:
- In a small bowl, mix together melted butter, granulated sugar, and ground cinnamon.

Brush the Topping:
- Once the pie is done baking, brush the melted butter, sugar, and cinnamon mixture over the top for a delicious finish.

Cool:
- Allow the Cinnamon Apple Crustless Pie to cool for a bit before slicing.

Serve:
- Slice and serve warm or at room temperature. Optionally, serve with a scoop of vanilla ice cream or a dollop of whipped cream.

This Cinnamon Apple Crustless Pie is a comforting and fuss-free dessert that highlights the natural sweetness of apples and the warmth of cinnamon. It's perfect for fall or anytime you crave the flavors of a classic apple pie without the crust. Enjoy making and savoring this delightful dessert!

www.ingramcontent.com/pod-product-compliance
Lightning Source LLC
LaVergne TN
LVHW062051070526
838201LV00080B/2292